U.S. Fish & Wildlife Service

Sport Fish and Wildlife Restoration and Associated Grant Programs

Program Update September 2006

Including a Special Highlight Section of the Mountain-Prairie Region

I0450434

Table of Contents

Comments from Assistant Director for Sport Fish and Wildlife Restoration Programs

Rowan Gould

Since joining the Federal Assistance program this spring, I am renewing long-standing partnerships and forming new relationships with supporters of the Wildlife and Sport Fish Restoration Programs. I am truly impressed with the complexity of our mission and with the wide support we enjoy from our partners. This Update provides a detailed report on the myriad of projects and their progress toward achieving Program goals and further highlight the marvelous job that the Federal Assistance is doing to encourage and foster partnerships. The key word is "partnership." Partners are becoming increasingly more important and integral to restoring and enhancing fish and wildlife and the habitats upon which they depend.

Prime examples are found in the challenges of implementing approved State Wildlife Action Plans. Implementation will require not only the concerted effort of the States and the Service, but also a willingness to seek out and secure the support from new partners. There are no boundaries on the partners that can and will be interested in cooperative conservation. Help from the conservation community, from members of industry and manufacturing firms, from scientists and academicians will be necessary. The skill sets from the traditional disciplines of natural resource management will be brought to bear on solving the identified conservation challenges in these Plans, as well as new talents needed to inform and engage the public in restoration plans and to monitor and track successes.

In the spirit of encouraging cooperative conservation, the Federal Assistance Program is helping to raise the visibility of approved plans, both within the Service as well as with other Federal Agencies. We welcome a wide distribution and application of the State Wildlife Action Plans to provide traditional and future cooperators with opportunities to assist in meeting Statewide and regional goals and to leverage limited resources to reach common goals. The synergy is exciting to contemplate and we are committed to facilitating such new opportunities.

In the spirit of fostering cooperative conservation through the grant programs funded through the Wildlife and Sport Fish Restoration Programs, we are setting the stage for preparing a Strategic Plan for the Wildlife and Sport Fish Restoration Programs. We will explore new ways to create efficiencies in delivery, and to enhance confidence in (and support for) the quality of grants management in the Service. We look forward to providing a road map to the future for the Wildlife and Sport Fish Restoration Programs—a road map that benefits from diverse perspectives, fresh ideas and deliberative suggestions.

I sincerely look forward to meeting the challenges of cooperative conservation through the Wildlife and Sport Fish Restoration Programs. Let me start on that path by welcoming you to engage with us by taking in the accomplishments we proudly display in this Program Update. I look forward to hearing the thoughts and ideas that come to mind as you consider these Programs, their delivery and their contributions to benefiting sport fish and wildlife resources.

facing page photo: Wineinger-Davis Ranch, Lincoln County, Colorado

Comments from Regional Director, Mountain-Prairie Region 6

Mitch King

Regional Director, Mitch King together with Rob Olson of Delta Waterfowl and Roger Holevoat, Project Leader on the Devil's Lake Wetland Management District during a field review of this WMD in North Dakota. USFWS

facing page photo: Lake Dillon, Summit County, Colorado

This edition of the Federal Assistance Program Update highlights the U.S. Fish and Wildlife Service's Mountain-Prairie Region which includes the States of Colorado, Kansas, Montana, Nebraska, North Dakota, South Dakota, Utah and Wyoming. This Region contains a diverse variety of habitats and landscapes which capture the mind and soul of the observer. The Region stretches from the banks of the Missouri River west to the desert border of Utah, from the prairies of Kansas north to the Canadian border of North Dakota and Montana. The Region contains such beauty as captured in "America the Beautiful" written by Katharine Lee Bates in 1893 while on a trip to Colorado Springs, Colorado, from the top of Pike's Peak. She said, "All the wonder of America seemed displayed there, with the sea-like expanse." The view was so beautiful that it inspired her to write the song that is considered by some to be the country's unofficial national anthem. Remember the words, "Oh beautiful for spacious skies, for amber waves of grain, for purple mountains majesty above the fruited plains…" this is the Mountain-Prairie Region.

The Region encompasses approximately 20 percent of the total land mass of the contiguous U.S. According to the Service's 2001 National Survey, over 10.2 million residents of the Region participate in wildlife recreation activities (about 74 percent of the population).

It is an outdoor enthusiast's dream come true with a unique and dynamic array of wildlife and sport fish opportunities. Watching bald eagles soar along the front range of the Rockies, seeing pronghorn antelope dash up to 60 miles per hour in the grasslands, listening to the croaking of toads in playa lakes filled after a thunderstorm, and being enchanted at the stable footing of bighorn sheep and mountain goats along cliffs are just part of the experiences that await visitors. Fishing for native trout in clear, clean mountain creeks and rivers, and angling for largemouth bass, walleye and other warm water fish in the numerous man-made reservoirs, makes the Region a recreation paradise for residents and tourists alike. Elk, mule deer and white tailed deer attract thousands of hunters to Colorado, Wyoming, Montana and Utah. Hunting birds such as quail, dove and pheasant brings joy to thousands of hunters in North and South Dakota, Nebraska and Kansas. Amphibians, birds, fish, mammals and reptiles that coexist in complex and diverse habitats and trophic relationships are diverse and plentiful. There are 56 listed species and 30 candidate species in the region including the bald eagle, black-footed ferret, gray wolf, grizzly bear, lynx, and pallid sturgeon.

The Mountain-Prairie Region is committed to fulfilling its responsibilities to its trust resources and the American people through partnerships. The Division of Federal Assistance works

Regional Director, Mitch King and Rob Olson, President of Delta Waterfowl viewing Gadwall eggs on the Devil's Lake Wetlands Management District in North Dakota. This is an example of the Regional Directors commitment to Partnerships. USFWS

closely with the 8 States, 37 Federally recognized tribes, and others to make resources available through 9 grant programs:

1. Pittman-Robertson Wildlife Restoration Act, with Hunter Education grants;
2. Dingell-Johnson Sport Fish Restoration Act, with Aquatic Education grants;
3. Endangered Species Grant Program;
4. Clean Vessel Act Program;
5. State Wildlife Grant Program;
6. Landowner Incentive Program;
7. Tribal Wildlife Grant Program;
8. Tribal Landowner Incentive Program;
9. Boating Infrastructure Grant Program.

These grants provide aquatic and hunter education; hunting and fishing opportunities; boating access; habitat acquisition and protection of habitat through fee title acquisition and conservation easements; access for hunting and wildlife watching through walk-in programs with private landowners; production of sport fish in State hatcheries; surveys and research on fish and wildlife species; technical guidance, planning and coordination; habitat creation and restoration efforts for species enhancement; and recovery of endangered and threatened species. The Service's grant programs assist each State or Tribe achieve its own objectives while contributing to national conservation goals.

In the Mountain-Prairie Region, there is a significant difference in the amount of private versus public land ownership. The Great Plains States of North Dakota, South Dakota, Nebraska, and Kansas have a greater percentage of private lands (up to 90 percent in North and South Dakota), and thus, rely on private landowners for wildlife habitat and populations. The Rocky Mountain States of Montana, Wyoming, Colorado and Utah have a significantly greater public land ownership. In these States, about 60 percent of all land ownership is private. The immense 40 percent of public lands offers vast resources for wildlife and the American public. The Landowner Incentive program, the State Wildlife program and their component Tribal programs, along with Endangered Species grants provide the Service with unparalleled opportunities and challenges to work with States, Tribal and local governments; and private landowners to benefit the diverse array of "species of greatest conservation need." Species of greatest conservation need are determined by the States. Examples include the greater sage grouse, Utah prairie dog, leatherside chub, Northern leopard frog and the Gila monster.

There are 37 Federally recognized tribes in the Region with an estimated population of 204,234 persons living on 9,456,551 acres of tribal lands. Habitats found on reservations and tribal lands contain unique environments for wildlife. The legacy and relationship of plant and animal communities to tribal cultures are significant. The Division of Federal Assistance works with the Region's Tribal Liaison to fund and administer projects proposed by Native American communities and Tribes. Since the creation of the Tribal Wildlife Grant and Tribal Landowner Incentive Program grant programs in 2002, 44 competitive grants have been awarded to 19 Tribes, in the amount of $8 million.

In this publication, you will read about some of the activities and accomplishments funded through the Division of Federal Assistance. I am proud of the partnerships that have been made in the Region among the Service, the States and the Tribes. We look forward to creating new partnerships and improving on existing partnerships for the positive needs of fish and wildlife and the people who use and enjoy these resources.

News Section

New Leadership and New Employees at the Washington Office

Pam Matthes was selected in April as the Deputy to both the Assistant Director for Migratory Birds and to the Assistant Director for Wildlife and Sport Fish Restoration Programs. She comes to both these programs after having served in the Division of Federal Assistance as special assistant to the Division Chief and also the Multistate Conservation Grant Program Coordinator.

Pam Matthes has worked among a wide variety of natural resource management programs throughout the U.S. Fish and Wildlife Service (FWS), the National Park Service (NPS) and the Department to protect and restore sensitive fish and wildlife habitat affected by special projects. Pam began her career with the FWS by working in the Office of Biological Services, which later became known as Ecological Services, where she served as a Fish and Wildlife Biologist providing protective stipulations governing oil and gas development on the outer continental shelf. Pam used knowledge gained in ES and moved to the Division of Refuge Management, where she designed protective stipulations governing the development of private oil and gas rights in select units of the National Wildlife Refuge System. She also worked on special projects, such as geothermal exploration in the Arctic NWR. While in Refuges, Pam also worked on significant land exchanges affecting units of both the National Wildlife Refuge System and the National Park System in Alaska.

From her work in Refuges, Pam joined the NPS where she assisted Park Superintendents with protecting natural resources during energy development of privately owned mineral rights. She later joined the Water Resources Division to enhance the wetlands protection and natural resource damage assessment programs of the NPS.

During her last year with the NPS and before returning to the FWS, Pam was the Special Assistant to the Assistant Secretary for Fish and Wildlife and Parks and assisted the National Park Service in strengthening its scientific capabilities to manage fish and wildlife resources in parks. During her time in the Assistant Secretary's Office, Pam secured legislative protection for the hydrothermal resources of Crater Lake National Park from adjacent geothermal development, for which she was awarded the Department's Honor Award for Superior Service.

After serving nearly 3 years as the Deputy Chief of the Division of Federal Assistance (FA), **Jim Greer** was announced as the new Chief, replacing Kris LaMontagne who retired in March of 2006. Prior to coming to the Washington Office he served as a Branch Chief in the FA program in Region 1 (Portland, Oregon). He came to the Service following 26 years working for the Oregon Department of Fish and Wildlife (ODFW). After a 10 year stint in the field as a wildlife biologist, Jim was promoted to the ODFW headquarters office and served as the Wildlife Division Chief for 5 years. In 1997 he was selected as the agency Director. In that capacity, and as a member of the Service Regulations Committee, Pacific Flyway Council, and President of the Western Association of Fish and Wildlife Agencies he worked closely with the Service on waterfowl issues, listings of salmon, trout and various nongame species, and addressing landscape level habitat protection issues.

"It's and honor to be selected as the Chief of Federal Assistance," Greer said. "This program has come a long way in the last several years and is now looked to for its expert knowledge and understanding of complex grants management issues and having a very efficient and effective business model that has stood the test of countless audits and review procedures. Our role in delivering over $600 million annually in grants to State Fish and Wildlife Agencies for conservation activities throughout the country is a huge responsibility. Our team of managers, biologists, support staff and grant, fiscal, training and IT specialists continue to provide excellent service and stand ready to take on new challenges at both the regional and Washington Office levels."

In May 2006, **John Stemple** assumed the position of the Multistate Conservation Grant Program coordinator within the Federal Assistance Division Washington Office.

John earned a Bachelor of Science degree in biology from the University of Pittsburgh and completed a Master's Degree in fisheries biology from the University of Rhode Island with additional core course work in oceanography.

He began his Federal career working as a biologist for the U.S. Forest Service at the Southeastern Forest Experiment Station, University of Virginia, Blacksburg, Virginia, surveying cold water streams for fish populations and habitat in the southern Appalachian Mountains including Great Smoky Mountains National Park in 1992. In addition, he worked as a volunteer fishery biologist for the Virginia Department of Game and Inland Fisheries doing similar work.

In 1993, he worked as a fishery biologist for the National Marine Fisheries Service, Habitat and Protected Resources Division in Oxford, Maryland. He served on several workgroups, such as Fish Passage, Habitat Restoration, and Submerged Aquatic Vegetation for the Chesapeake Bay Program. In 2001, he began his career with the USFWS at the Athens, GA Ecological Services Field Office. His major duties included FERC hydropower and DOT project review. He also provided technical guidance in stream morphology, description, erosion control and fish habitat improvement.

In June, 2002, he assumed responsibilities as a FWS fishery biologist/grant manager under the Federal Assistance Grants program in the Atlanta Regional Office. He coordinated approximately 75 Sport Fish Restoration grants among five States in the Southeast and acted as program manager for the Coastal Wetlands Conservation Grant program.

Tom McCoy joined the Division in August 2006 as staff to the Policy Branch. His responsibilities will include updating Service manual chapters and regulations. He graduated from Columbus State University 1996, with a B.S. in Biological Science and completed course work toward a M.S. in Environmental Science in 2002.

Tom began his career in 1996, at Mead Coated Board (Mead-Westvaco) Woodlands Division as a Forestry/GIS technician where he performed GIS field work, installed research plots while cruising timber, and researched deer populations and forage preference in Alabama. In 1999, Tom relocated to the City of Griffin, Georgia where he worked as an Environmental Technician/Urban Forester. While in Griffin, he dealt with water quality and environmental issues related to construction and stormwater, as well as reviewing and inspecting site plans.

His urban forestry duties included the inspection and maintenance of 12,000 city trees, writing the city's tree ordinance, and serving as a member of the tree board. In 2001, Tom took a position as the Land Condition Trend Analysis coordinator at Fort Benning, Georgia where he inventoried and monitored Army training land resources such as vegetation, avian, faunal, and soil studies.

He provided the installation with technical expertise from his findings such as summary reports, monthly reports, briefings, meetings, and presentations to support land management decisions. In early 2002, he also assumed the responsibilities of the GIS Program Analyst, providing maps for the installation using ArcGIS and ArcView. In June 2002, Tom accepted a wildlife biologist position with the USFWS Division of Federal Assistance-Southeast Region in Atlanta, Georgia where he manages the technical overview of grant programs for 5 States in the region. He also manages all Hunter Education Program Grants for the Region and conducts technical reviews and processing of projects from State grantees receiving Federal Assistance Funds (under Pittman-Robertson Wildlife Restoration Act, Dingell-Johnson Sport Fish Restoration Act, State Wildlife Grants, Landowner Incentive Program, Endangered Species Act, and Wildlife Conservation and Restoration Program) to ensure that these projects are substantial in character and design and in accordance with the Federal Assistance Manual, Policy Statements, Executive Orders, and Office of Management and Budget Circulars.

Tom has been married for 4 years and has an 18-month-old son. Tom's hobbies include hunting and fishing, golf, baseball/softball, video games, and spending time with his wife and son.

Christy Kuczak with a green sea turtle, Chelonia mydas, that is nesting in Singer Island, Florida.

Christy Kuczak has also joined the Federal Assistance Washington Office. She will serve as a grants management specialist in the Branch of Grant Operations and Policy. Christy comes to us from the U.S. Department of Agriculture in the Cooperative State Research, Education, and Extension Service (CSREES) where she was a Program Specialist. She managed formula and competitive grant programs for research, education, and extension primarily at Land Grant Universities around the U.S., including the Historically Black Universities and Colleges, Tribal Colleges, and Hispanic Serving Institutions. While at CSREES, she specialized in programs in the natural resources area, with most of her work focusing on programs in forestry, sustainable development, ecology, rangeland management, fish and wildlife. Her experience in strategic planning, the PART process, facilitation, and building partnerships will likely carry over into her duties with FWS. She received various awards for her work related to diversity, strategic planning, and electronic grants. She has an M.S. in Soil and Crop Sciences from Cornell University with her thesis work on agroforestry systems and the influence of agroforestry trees and large earthworms on soil fertility of the Brazilian Amazon. She also earned a B.S. in Environmental and Plant Biology from Ohio University.

Staff Directory
Federal Assistance

Washington DC Office

Federal Assistance Main Phone Number
703/358 2156

Web Address
http://federalaid.fws.gov

Rowan Gould, Assistant Director for Wildlife and Sport Fish Restoration Programs

Pam Matthes, Deputy Assistant Director for Migratory Birds and Wildlife and Sport Fish Restoration

Jim Greer, Division Chief

Vacant, Deputy Division Chief - Operations

Doug Gentile, Civil Rights Coordinator for Public Access

Jimmye Kane, Lead Secretary

John Stemple, Multistate Conservation Grants Coordinator

Vacant, Secretary

Branch of Budget and Administration
Tom Jeffrey, Branch Chief - Budget Development and Execution - Program Management

Mary Grieco, Administrative Officer

Vacant, Program Support Assistant

Vacant, Program Analyst

Branch of Information Management
Lori Bennett, Branch Chief

Vacant, Fiscal Management - Audit Liaison

Ed Duda, System Developer

Michele Storz, IT Specialist

Jeffrey Graves, Server Support - Web Site Support

Pete Hitchcock, Network Engineer, Security Officer

C. J. Huang, Database Administrator

Sandie Lehberger, Administrative Technician

David Washington, ADP Systems Support - ADP Acquisition Support

Debbie Wircenske, Help Desk, Quality Assurance, Fiscal Administration and Training

Luther Zachary, FAIMS Branch Chief

Branch of Grants Operations and Policy
Tom Barnes, Branch Chief

Brian Bohnsack, Sport Fish Restoration, Clean Vessel Act - Boating Infrastructure Grants

Kim Galvan, Regulations - Support staff for Joint Federal/State Task Force for Federal Assistance

Genevieve Pullis-LaRouche, State Wildlife Grants - Landowner Incentive Program

Christy Kuczak, Coastal Wetlands

Tom McCoy, Federal Assistance Manual Review, Rulemaking

Branch of Audits
Vacant, Branch Chief - Audits

Ord Bargerstock, Acting Branch Chief, Systems Accountant - Audit Resolution

Branch of Surveys
Sylvia Cabrera, Branch Chief - National Survey of Fishing, Hunting and Wildlife-Associated Recreation

Richard Aiken, Economist - National Survey

Jerry Leonard, Economist - National Survey

Branch of Training
Steve Leggans, Branch Chief

Julie Schroyer, Administrative Analyst

Debbie Unbehagen, Grants Management Specialist (Instructor)

Scott Knight, Grants Management Specialist (Instructor)

Federal Assistance Program Overview

The goal of the Federal Assistance program is to work with States to conserve, protect, and enhance fish, wildlife, their habitats, and the hunting, sport fishing, and recreational boating opportunities they provide. The Federal Assistance Program is responsible for administering the following Programs:

- Wildlife Restoration
- Sport Fish Restoration
- Clean Vessel Act
- Boating Infrastructure Grants
- National Coastal Wetlands Conservation Grants

- Multistate Conservation Grants
- State Wildlife Grants
- Landowner Incentive
- Hunter Education and Safety Program

In addition, Federal Assistance provides grant management support for endangered species traditional section 6, Habitat Conservation Plan (HCP) Land Acquisition, HCP Planning, and Recovery Land Acquisition grant programs. The following is an update on the accomplishments of the Federal Assistance program and its partners with these grant programs.

Focus on Specific Programs and Activities

Landowner Incentive Program

In August, 39 State and territorial wildlife agencies were notified that they would receive a 2006 LIP grant. Of these States, 37 received a Tier I grant to help initiate or improve existing efforts dealing with private lands. Individual Tier I grants ranged in value from almost $69,000 to $180,000. Another 17 States received Tier II grants to help pay for specific projects. The value of Tier II grants varied from $436,000 to over $945,000.

Following 2007 budget deliberations, both the House and Senate Conference reported budgets that were much smaller than were requested in the President's budget. A final budget number will not be ready until the budget is approved, which may not be until the fall or winter of 2006. In light of potentially reduced funding, Federal Assistance personnel have worked to determine the most effective and equitable ways to rank projects and distribute funds. These changes are being incorporated into a Request For Proposals.

State Wildlife Grants

The review of the Wildlife Action Plans (aka Comprehensive Wildlife Conservation Strategies) is beginning to wind down. In February 2006, the National Advisory Acceptance Team (NAAT) completed the initial review of all 56 Plans. Of the initial submissions, 38 were approved as written and 18 were conditionally approved. Of those that were conditionally approved five have been resubmitted and approved, and two others have been resubmitted and will be reviewed early in August. If all goes well, the review process should be finished by December 2006.

In the meantime, the State Wildlife Grants program continues to mature. Federal Assistance personnel in the Washington Office and the Regions continue to assist the States in their efforts to implement the Plans. Personnel have been involved in each of the multi-State coordination efforts organized by the regional associations of the Association of Fish and Wildlife Agencies (AFWA). Likewise, Federal Assistance personnel, working with the AFWA, have been actively involved in promoting the use of the Plans by other Federal agencies, such as the Department of Defense and the Natural Resources Conservation Service and within the Service Federal Assistance personnel continue to provide guidance to other programs as they work to integrate these documents into their operations.

During April 2006, a workgroup was formed to update the State Wildlife Grants program guidelines. This team, which represents the Service and the State wildlife agencies, has been reviewing the historic guidelines, adapting text to represent current situations, and drafting new guidelines to address issues that hadn't occurred when the original guidelines were drafted. State agencies had the opportunity to discuss the draft guidelines at the "One Year Later" meeting at NCTC during the first week of August 2006, and the draft text was made available on Group Systems shortly thereafter so State agencies could provide official input. The final guidelines should be available by the Association of Fish and Wildlife Agencies' Annual Conference in September 2006.

Fiscal Year 2007 National Coastal Wetlands Grant Program Funding Proposals Under Consideration

The Service is currently evaluating proposals submitted for funding from the National Coastal Wetlands Conservation grant program for fiscal year 2007. The proposals are reviewed by a panel of Service personnel and this group's funding recommendations are forwarded on to the Director for consideration. The program's awards are expected to be announced in early December after the final receipts into the Sport Fish Restoration and Boating Trust Fund are determined for fiscal year 2006.

The Service estimates that approximately $16 million will be available for proposals in fiscal year 2007. Thirty-three proposals from 14 States requesting a total of $24.1 million of Federal funding for fiscal year 2007.

Almost $208 million in awards from the National Coastal Wetlands Conservation grant program have been awarded since its inception in the early 1990s. The program is credited with the acquisition, protection and restoration of thousands of acres of critical coastal wetlands habitat.

Boating Infrastructure Grant Program Improvements Continue

The Service continues to refine and improve the administration of the Boating Infrastructure Grant program. Several notable changes were made to the program in fiscal year 2006 as the Service implemented program improvements recommended by the Sport Fishing and Boating Partnership Council. Some of these improvements included delaying the initial deadline for proposals to October 31 in order to allow boating interests more time to prepare proposals and to remove some of the pressure of proposal preparation during the peak boating season. The Service released Tier 1 funds much earlier in this grant cycle than in previous years. Specifically, the Service released the funds to States as proposals were received, rather than waiting until the announcement of the Tier 2 awards. Additionally, Service staff and members of the Sport Fishing and Boating Partnership Council's Boating Infrastructure Grant Program committee met jointly to review and rank Tier 2 proposals for the first time since the program's inception. The joint ranking of proposals resulted in improved efficiency in the proposal selection process, while increasing the partnership between the Service and its stakeholders.

The Service intends to continue to refine the program in the coming year and to implement additional recommendations made by the Sport Fishing and Boating Partnership Council. The Service is accepting proposals for the fiscal year 2007 grant cycle through October 31.

Other program highlights for fiscal year 2006 included awarding $3.7 million of Tier 1 funds to 38 States, including $100,000 which was awarded to the Arizona for its first ever participation in the program. The Service received 30 proposals requesting a total of $21.5 million for the Tier 2 funds in fiscal year 2006. The Service was able to award $8,280,596 in Tier 2 awards this fiscal year. Funding for the program increased approximately $3 million this fiscal year as a result of the funding changes passed by Congress in the Safe, Accountable, Flexible, Efficient Transportation Equity Act (P.L. 109-059). The Tier 2 proposals receiving funding included:

Alabama: The Decatur Riverwalk Marina Transient Facilities, the City of Decatur and the Riverwalk Marina, LLC, will receive $236,127 and match $327,117 to construct a total of 20 transient boat slips for boaters using Wheeler Reservoir on the Tennessee River.

California: The Camp Emerald Bay Improvements on Santa Catalina Island will receive $445,000 and match $523,500 to construct a floating dock and dinghy dock.

Marina Del Rey, The Harbor Real Estate Group, The Boatyard and several cooperators will receive $825,000 and match $2,235,000 to modernize a dilapidated fuel dock to a state-of-the-art facility.

The Pier 38 Maritime Recreation Center in San Francisco will receive $1,500,000 and match $2,714,890 to construct a fuel dock and additional floating docks for transient boaters. The project is estimated to double the amount of transient dockage available in the local area.

The Westpoint Marina and Boat Yard in Redwood City will receive $693,153 and match $693,153 to construct new floating docks with utilities providing accommodations for up to 48 transient boats. This will improve facilities for transient boaters in the South San Francisco Bay area.

Maine: Camden Harbor Wharf Renovation will receive $300,000 and match $900,605 to repair a fuel dock wharf area and fund one-time dredging and the installation of 20 new transient slips.

Maryland: The Baltimore Inner Harbor Marine Center will receive $1,080,577 and match $1,124,683 to reconstruct the existing marina to provide 92 slips for transient boats.

New Jersey: The Key Harbor Transient Facilities in Waretown will receive $321,582 and match $172,105 to construct twelve transient slips with amenities through the installation of a bulkhead. Key Harbor Marina is centrally located to Long Beach Island and Tuckerton Seaport.

The Sandy Hook Bay Marina Transient Facilities in Borough of Highlands will receive $611,664 and match $611,661 to construct 32 transient slips by relocating the marina entrance and provide utilities for these sites.

New York: The Eagle Creek Marina in Kendall will receive $245,741 and match $267,765 to construct 24 new transient slips with utilities, add new restrooms, and install an updated sewage system and fuel dock for transient boaters at the Eagle Creek Marina.

Oregon: The Gleason Transient Tie-up and Wave Wall will receive $820,800 and match $461,700 to protect and improve the existing moorage for transient boaters at the M. James Gleason Boat Ramp, a major boating site on the Columbia River.

The Maple Street Transient Tie-up in Florence will receive $480,000 and match $370,000 to replace the aging transient docks located in the historic waterfront of Old Town. Approximately 270 feet of new concrete floats will be constructed to provide transient boaters access to this popular area.

The Sandy Beach on Government Island in the Columbia River will receive $544,000 and match $316,000 to complete the development of the Sandy Beach boat-only access.

Texas: Port Lavaca will receive $176,452 and match $75,623 to construct new boat slips for transient boaters. Specifically, the project will add 200 linear feet with 6 fingers to provide 12 new boats slips with electrical and water hookups.

Clean Vessel Act Grant Program Being Evaluated

Service Director Dale Hall has charged the Sport Fishing and Boating Partnership Council to complete an assessment of the Clean Vessel Act Grant program. The review began over the summer and is expected to last approximately 1 year. The review will be similar to the Council's assessment of the Boating Infrastructure Grant program which was completed in 2005. Some of the items to be assessed include the program's funding practices. Boating stakeholders on the Council had expressed an interest and willingness to assess the program, which has been in existence since the early 1990s. Congress reauthorized the program as part of the Safe, Accountable, Flexible, Efficient Transportation Equity Act (P.L. 109-059). The program is credited with improving the water quality in many parts of the country and program participants have installed thousands of sewage pumpout stations throughout the country. In addition, program participants have purchased hundreds of sewage pumpout boats and States' educational programs inform thousands of individuals each year about proper sewage disposal.

The Service awarded $12.26 million to 32 States from the 2006 Clean Vessel Act grant program for fiscal year 2006 earlier this summer. The Service received 42 proposals from 32 States requesting a total of $18.1 million of Federal funds from the Clean Vessel Act program in fiscal year 2006. The Service awarded all available funds to grant recipients. A summary of the awards and recipients include:

Alabama- $255,604- The State plans to install 24 sewage pumpout stations and purchase 2 sewage pumpout boats for its inland and coastal waters. These facilities and boats are planned for use on areas such as the Dog River, Mobile Bay, Wheeler Lake and Lake Martin. In addition, the State plans to continue its efforts to inform boaters about the importance of proper sewage disposal.

Arkansas- $79,600- The State plans to install 4 new sewage pumpout facilities and purchase 3 sewage pumpout boats. These facilities are planned for Greer's Ferry Lake, Table Rock Lake, Lake Ouachita, Bull Shoals Lake, and Lake Norfork. In addition, the State will continue with its efforts to inform boaters about the importance of proper sewage disposal.

Arizona- $105,683- The State will renovate the 1 public pumpout station on Lake Havasu and install a new pumpout facility at Lake Pleasant.

California- $1,383,895- The State plans to construct sewage pumpout facilities and floating restrooms, as well as purchase 4 sewage pumpout boats with its program awards. These facilities and boats are planned throughout the State in its inland and coastal waters. The State will also continue its educational program for recreational boaters.

Connecticut- $988,652- The State plans to construct 2 sewage pumpout stations and purchase 2 sewage pumpout boats. In addition, the State will continue its education program for recreational boaters and also assist with the operation and maintenance of approximately 40

sewage pumpout facilities and 15 sewage pumpout boats throughout the State's coastal areas.

Delaware- $157,700- The State plans to construct 6 sewage pumpout stations for the coastal areas and to continue its education program for recreational boaters.

Georgia- $27,969- The State plans to assist with the development of a sewage pumpout facility at Trade Winds marina on Strom Thurmond Lake.

Florida- $1,335,570- The State plans to construct sewage pumpout facilities in both its coastal and inland waters, as well as continuing its education program to inform boaters about the importance of proper sewage disposal. The majority of the award ($1,000,000) will be used in the State's coastal waters.

Hawaii- $1,000,000- The State plans to develop sewage pumpout facilities at Port Allen and Maalaea Small Boat Harbors and to continue its educational program for recreational boaters.

Idaho- $49,851- The State plans to develop a new sewage pumpout facility at Priest Lake near the city of Coolin.

Illinois- $50,000- The State plans to construct up to 5 sewage pumpout facilities at private marinas in its inland waters.

Indiana- $104,458- The State plans to construct 4 sewage pumpout stations throughout the State and to continue its education program for recreational boaters. Two of the new stations are proposed for either the Ohio River or Lake Michigan waters.

Kentucky- $74,377- The State plans to construct up to 4 sewage pumpout stations and continue its education program to inform recreational boaters about the importance of proper sewage disposal. The State plans to put 2 new pumpout facilities on Herrington Lake and at Craig's Creek on the Ohio River.

Louisiana- $333,000- The State plans to develop as many as 7 sewage pumpout facilities throughout the State. These include 6 in coastal areas and 1 in inland waters. The State will continue its education with recreational boaters.

Maine- $294,920- The State plans to construct as many as 10 sewage pumpout stations at private and public marinas and to provide operation and

maintenance funds for pumpout stations previously installed with Clean Vessel Act program funds. The State will also continue its efforts to educate boaters about the importance of proper sewage disposal.

Maryland- $655,000- The State plans to install 17 new sewage pumpout stations and replace or upgrade 12 existing facilities in coastal waters. Additionally, the State will continue its education program for recreational boaters and will also provide operations and maintenance funds for facilities previously installed with Clean Vessel Act program funds.

Massachusetts- $1,000,000- The State plans to renovate or install new sewage pumpout stations at 10 facilities along the coast including in Plum Island Sound and Salem Sound. Grant funds will also be used to replace up to 7 motors on sewage pumpout boats. The State will also continue its education program for recreational boaters.

Michigan- $200,000- The State plans to install as many as 10 sewage pumpout stations at private marinas throughout the Great Lakes. Additionally the State plans to continue its educational program for recreational boaters.

Minnesota- $29,206- The State plans to install a new sewage pumpout station on the St. Croix River in Washington County.

Missouri- $36,000- The State plans to install 3 new sewage pumpout facilities throughout the State and to continue its effort to inform recreational boaters about the importance of proper sewage disposal.

Nevada- $16,452- The State plans to assist with the installation of a new sewage pumpout facility at the Las Vegas Boat Harbor on Lake Mead.

New Hampshire- $131,175- The State plans to install 2 new sewage pumpout facilities including one at either Lake Winnipesaukee or Lake Sunapee, as well as providing operation and maintenance funding for other facilities installed previously with program funds. The State will also continue its educational program for recreational boaters.

Ohio- $173,224- The State plans to install 2 new sewage pumpout facilities. One is planned for the Chagrin River near the town of Eastlake and 1 is planned for a marina on Lake Erie near Cleveland. The State will also continue its efforts to

educate boaters about the importance of proper sewage disposal.

Oklahoma- $17,784- The State will install a new pumpout facility at Lake Murray.

Oregon- $393,160- The State plans to install as many as 15 sewage pumpout stations and one floating restroom throughout the State's coastal and inland waters. The State also plans to continue its efforts to educate boaters about the importance of proper sewage disposal.

Rhode Island- $384,000- The State plans to install 21 new sewage pumpout facilities and purchase a sewage pumpout boat. The State will also continue its educational program for recreational boaters.

Tennessee- $239,011- The State plans to install sewage pumpout stations primarily in the Mississippi, Tennessee and Cumberland River systems throughout the State. In addition, the State will continue its efforts to educate boaters about the importance of proper sewage disposal.

Texas- $771,351- The State will construct 6 sanitary pumpout facilities for recreational boating at coastal marina facilities, renovate 6 existing restrooms, construct 4 new restrooms located adjacent to coastal public boat ramps and continue a boater education program regarding waste disposal. In addition, the State plans to pursue partnerships with local governments and other State agencies to provide pumpout facilities where there are already water-based recreation opportunities such as parks, marinas or boat ramps

Utah- $105,000- The State plans to assist with the replacement of a sewage pumpout station at Cedar Springs Marina on Flaming Gorge Reservoir.

Virginia- $928,125- The State plans to install 28 sewage pumpout stations, 1 floating restroom and purchase 1 sewage pumpout boat for its inland and coastal waters. Additionally, the State will continue its efforts to educate boaters about the importance of proper disposal of their sewage.

Washington- $1,000,000- The State plans to install sewage pumpout facilities throughout the State on its inland and coastal waters. In addition, the State will continue its educational program for recreational boaters.

Wisconsin- $45,000- The State plans to install 3 sewage pumpout facilities on inland waters and the Great Lakes with the program awards.

The Service will announce the request for funding proposals for the fiscal year 2007 grant cycle later this year. Proposals will be due in early 2007.

State Audits

The Division of Federal Assistance is required to audit each State entity participating in the Sports Fish and Wildlife Restoration programs 2 of every 5 years. To conduct the audits, we have contracted with the Department of the Interior, Office of Inspector General. Currently, there are 7 entities being audited in 6 States. The 6 States that are now in the fieldwork stage of audits are:

- Georgia
- Maine
- Maryland
- Missouri
- North Dakota
- South Carolina

We expect the audits to be completed on time by the end of the fiscal year.

The next 5-year cycle of State audits will begin October 2006. We will continue working with the Department of the Interior, Office of Inspector General for audit services.

The Division strives to maintain open lines of communication between the auditors, grantees, and Federal Assistance offices. All comments and suggestions on our audit program are welcome. Our experiences and the feedback from the audits continue to be very positive, and we look forward to our continued partnership with all of our stakeholders. For additional information on this issue, please contact Ord Bargerstock.

FAIMS/FBMS

The Federal Assistance Information Management System (FAIMS) is used by the Service to manage the complete life cycle of over half a billion dollars in grants annually. FAIMS was scheduled to be replaced by the Department of Interior's planned Financial Business Management System (FBMS) in Fiscal Year 2007. Problems encountered have lead to selection of a new system integrator and further delays in deployment. Implementation of the FBMS in the Fish and Wildlife Service is now scheduled for Fiscal Year 2010.

Required upgrades to modernize FAIMS infrastructure have been completed in order to facilitate continued vendor support and increase system security.

The system is now being subjected to a lengthy multistep security analysis process required for renewal of the system's Certification and Accreditation.

Luther Zachary, Chief Branch of FAIMS Support, has been designated as System Manager. The designation was formerly held by Lori Bennett, Chief of Information Management.

Work continues on:
1. Refinement of internal controls for FAIMS maintenance, testing and operations.
2. Refinements to the FAIMS Land module required to increase ease of use and eliminate bugs.
3. Improvements to various aspects of system security.

Multistate Conservation Grant Program

Multistate Conservation Grants are awarded cooperatively with the Association of Fish and Wildlife Agencies (AFWA). These grants support products and solve high priority problems affecting States on a regional or national basis and allow for efficient use of limited resources to address the national conservation needs of States established through the AFWA. Examples below highlight the broad array of projects supported by Multistate Conservation grants. To learn more about all projects funded and the benefits derived from the Multistate Conservation Grant Program, please visit http://faims.fws.gov.

Western Native Trout Initiative

The basic objective of this grant is to speed the implementation of conservation, management and information needs of native Western trout. With few exceptions, native trout populations have declined across the West, usually due to habitat alteration and introduced species that result in predation, competition, or hybridization. Because the native Western trout species occupy a number of watersheds, a broad scale conservation strategy will be necessary to achieve the objective. These watersheds often span a number of jurisdictions, therefore, a cooperative joint venture strategy involving Federal, State, tribal and local governments, conservation and recreational organizations, private landowners and individual citizens to produce a management plan will be necessary. At project completion this grant will provide for improved coordination, and a unified approach to conservation by the partners to improve the status of populations and habitats of Western native trout. The end result will be improved recreational opportunities for anglers across the Western States.

International Instream Flow Program Initiative

The majority of State and Provincial fish and wildlife agencies have historically managed fisheries for the most part by regulation, stocking, and physical habitat management and restoration. While these strategies are integral parts of fisheries management, the greatest gains in fish management in the future will occur as result of protecting, restoring, and managing water for aquatic habitats. The comments of 4 State fish and wildlife agency fishery chiefs in the March 2005 issue of *Bass Times* magazine support this fact as do conclusions of the National Fish Habitat Initiative, and the American Fisheries Society workshop in Milwaukee, that identified securing adequate instream flow and water volumes as one of the 10 greatest challenges to fish habitat.

The overall goal of this project is to enhance fish habitat at State/Provincial, regional, and national levels by identifying water management trends and opportunities that will help State and Provincial fishery and wildlife management agencies develop, maintain, or improve their instream flow and water management programs and effectiveness. Regardless of the present level of instream flow and water management expertise within any one agency's organization, this project will provide a clear awareness of where their program has been, what their capabilities are today, and what opportunities exist for improving their programs. By integrating the input of instream flow experts from all States and Provinces, the project will allow participating agencies to develop strategies and solutions that reflect the unique opportunities that may exist at State/Provincial, regional, and national levels.

Sage-Grouse Interstate Working Group Coordinator

The objective of this grant is to continue funding a full-time position to coordinate and facilitate interstate conservation planning, inventory, research, and management actions to conserve sage-grouse populations range wide. The sage-grouse range covers millions of acres in 11 Western States and 2 Canadian Provinces. Population declines and loss of range have prompted concern for the species by the Western Association of Fish and Wildlife Agencies, Bureau of Land Management, U.S. Forest Service and the U.S. Fish and Wildlife Service. In July 2000 these agencies developed a National Framework Team, as part of an interagency Memorandum of Understanding, to guide and coordinate the species' conservation. This proposal will help provide the staffing necessary to implement the provisions of the MOU. An anticipated outcome will be the production of a coordinated, cooperative strategy for advancing conservation and preservation of sage-grouse and their range.

Greater sage grouse. USFWS

The National Federal Assistance Training Program

The National Federal Assistance Training Program, located at the National Conservation Training Center in Shepherdstown, WV, is part of the Washington Office of Federal Assistance. The training program develops and delivers grants management training for Federal Assistance staff and State fish and wildlife agency grantees. These training courses increase the knowledge, skills and abilities of State and Federal personnel who manage Federal assistance grants. This training helps to ensure that Federal assistance grant managers consistently apply the laws, rules, and policies that govern Federal assistance program administration.

Since 1996, almost 1,800 State and Federal assistance grant managers and grantees have received training through courses and workshops developed by, or offered in cooperation with, the Federal Assistance Training Program.

Training offered includes: Basic Grants Management Course, Project Leaders Course, Federal Assistance Audit Training, Grant Writing Workshop, Compliance Issues Workshop, and GroupSystems Leader Training. Online training modules covering an introduction to Federal assistance grant programs and processes and a familiarization to the Federal Assistance Toolkit are also available on the Federal Assistance Training Program Web site. An advanced grant management course covering fiscal, programmatic, and compliance issues is scheduled as a pilot course for October 2006.

Course descriptions, an on-line application, an on-line training request form, training materials, and other grant manager's resources are available on the Federal Assistance Training Program web site at: http://training.fws.gov/fedaid/.

For additional information contact Steve Leggans at the National Conservation Training Center at 304/876-7927.

National Survey of Fishing, Hunting, and Wildlife-Associated Recreation

The Census Bureau successfully completed the first wave of data collection for the 2006 FHWAR Survey on June 3. The second wave will be conducted in September and October 2006, and the third, and last, in January and February 2007.

The first wave included screening interviews of U.S. households to identify a sample of 31,500 sportspersons (anglers and hunters) and 24,300 wildlife watchers (observers, photographers, and feeders). It also included the first detailed interviews of sample persons who had already participated in wildlife-related recreation in 2006. They were asked questions about their activities and expenditures.

Over 1,000 Census interviewers contacted 85,000 households for the Screening Interviews and got a remarkable *89% response rate*! Most data were collected by computer-assisted telephone interviews. However, in-person interviews were conducted when individuals could not be reached by phone.

The Census Bureau also successfully completed the first wave of interviews in 3 States (Ohio, Missouri, and Washington) for a *Side-by-Side Test* to determine the feasibility of using State license databases as a sample source for future surveys. The same sportsperson questionnaire, time frame, and protocols—except for the sample source—were used for both the regular survey and the test sample. These data will be analyzed to determine the comparability of the test results with the regular survey results. The analysis will be completed in April 2007.

The 2006 survey will be the 11th conducted since 1955. The Service has coordinated the survey every 5 years at the request of State fish and wildlife agencies. The survey will be similar in content, scope, and methodology to those conducted in 1991, 1996, and 2001 so their estimates will be comparable.

The 2006 survey will generate information identified as priority data needed by the States, non-governmental organizations, and other major survey users. General categories of information collected include the number of participants in different types of fish and wildlife recreational activities, the extent of participation (days and trips), and related trip and equipment expenditures.

The 2006 survey is funded by Multistate Conservation grants from the Wildlife and Sport Fish Restoration programs. Products will include preliminary reports, a final national and 50 State reports, database CDs, and quick facts brochures. All data and reports will be available on the Fish and Wildlife Service's Web site.

A preliminary report with national information will be issued June 2007 and one with State data July 2007. A final national report will be available in October 2007, and State reports will be available on a flow basis starting in November.

The Service also produces analytical reports based on survey data. Addenda to the 2001 survey include the following 10 reports: *Birding in the United States: A Demographic and Economic Analysis*; *2001 National and State Economic Impacts of Wildlife Watching*; *Net Economic Values for Wildlife-Related Recreation in 2001*; *Participation and Expenditure Patterns of African-American, Hispanic, and Female Hunters and Anglers*; *Fishing and Hunting 1991-2001: Avid, Casual, and Intermediate Participation Trends*; *Deer Hunting in the United States: An Analysis of Hunter Demographics and Behavior*; *The Relationship between Wildlife Watchers, Hunters, and Anglers*; *Private and Public Land Use by Hunters*; and *Economic Impact of Waterfowl Hunting in the United States*.

Copies of survey reports are available on request or are accessible through the following Web site: http://federalaid.fws.gov. For more information you also may contact the Service's survey staff.

Special Highlight
Mountain-Prairie Region

Mountain-Prairie Region (CO, KS, MT, NE, ND, SD, UT, WY)

The U.S. Fish and Wildlife Service Mountain-Prairie Region is composed of the great States of Colorado, Kansas, Montana, Nebraska, North Dakota, South Dakota, Utah, and Wyoming. The habitats and fish and wildlife that use those habitats are as diverse as the Region's landscape. Rivers, lakes, mountains, prairies, desert, and more can be found in our great Region.

In fiscal year 2006, Region 6 Division of Federal Assistance provided approximately $81,356,627 in Federally apportioned funds to our Region's State fish and game departments to support hunting, angling, and non-consumptive wildlife user programs. We're proud of the work we are doing and invite you to take a look at some of our Region's highlights in this program update. Better yet, we invite everyone to visit our States to enjoy some of the best fish and wildlife experiences our country has to offer.

State Federal Assistance Coordinator's Annual Meeting in Saratoga, WY. Shown are all the State FA Coordinators and Regional Federal Assistance Staff.

State Wildlife Grant Program a Catalyst for Western States Partnership Effort

Sagebrush, shrub-steppe and prairie ecosystems are a defining part of the landscape and history of the American West. These ecosystems are an integral part of the richness of a diversity of Western cultures and groups. Native Americans, ranchers, hunters, and others enjoy myriad recreational opportunities and the beauty and vibrancy of the landscape. Many sensitive wildlife species also rely on these ecosystems: the pygmy rabbit, black-footed ferret, prairie dogs, sage thrasher, swift fox, lesser prairie chicken, Swainson's hawk, ferruginous hawk, mountain plover, to name just a few. The habitats in these ecosystems are life-sustaining for many game species, including mule deer, pronghorn antelope, and sage grouse.

A host of factors have combined to cause an alarming decline of the habitats of the sagebrush and prairie ecosystems. Human activities have contributed to the decadent and unhealthy conditions of these ecosystems: including land and energy development; disruption of normal fire cycles; improper grazing practices, brush control, and off-road vehicle use; and infestations of non-native plants. A prolonged drought has increased the severity of these effects. As a consequence, many of the species that depend on these habitats are becoming stressed and are being considered for listing under the Endangered Species Act.

In response, Western States are working to address threats to these ecosystems and their species to avert the need for Federal listing. Because these ecosystems range over great distances and across State borders, it benefits the States to engage in collaborative efforts. The State Wildlife Grant program is helping one multi-State effort, involving 8 Western States, to develop and implement conservation plans to maintain and enhance sagebrush and shrub-steppe ecosystems with a focus on Columbia sharp-tailed grouse and sage-grouse species. These planning and implementation processes are also engaging Federal and other State agencies, local governments, farmers, ranchers, nongovernmental organizations, and other partners.

The State Wildlife Grant program is also jump starting another multi-State effort to develop a comprehensive strategy for conserving shrub-steppe and prairie ecosystems across the Western Great Plains. Twelve Western States will work together to beef up conservation strategies for the white-tailed and Gunnison prairie dogs, develop State-specific prairie dog management plans, conduct surveys and inventories to obtain current information on the conditions and trends of the species and their habitats, and encourage participation with stakeholders and partners. The States will also collaborate with Canada and Mexico on mutual projects.

Colorado has completed a number of local and rangewide species and habitat conservation plans, management guidelines, and a best management practice guide. Colorado has also worked with a private landowner to protect 560 acres of Gunnison sage-grouse habitat with a conservation easement.

Utah has placed an emphasis on working with local communities with the philosophy that "If it's not good for communities, it's not good for wildlife."

Local working groups have been established for each of the 12 sage-grouse management units in Utah and most of these groups have completed conservation plans for their units. Utah also participated with other States to publish a rangewide assessment of factors affecting the health and trend of greater sage-grouse populations and habitats. Utah worked with the State of Colorado and number of Federal agencies to develop a rangewide conservation plan for the Gunnison sage-grouse. Members of the Utah Partners for Conservation and Development have agreed to share resources in an unprecedented initiative to conserve sagebrush ecosystems Statewide with a special emphasis on sage-grouse and mule deer habitats. The Utah Division of Wildlife Resources has hired 5 wildlife biologists to work throughout the State exclusively on protection and restoration of sagebrush and shrub-steppe habitats. In just 1 year, about 6,500 acres have undergone a number of habitat enhancement projects, including prescribed burns, planting of seedlings, livestock fencing, and sagebrush manipulation.

Under the Landowner Incentive Program, Montana is implementing the Sagebrush Initiative to achieve long-term protection of 183,000 acres of privately owned key sagebrush/grassland habitats in Montana. The Initiative will provide incentive payments to private landowners to voluntarily refrain from sodbusting and sagebrush control to allow conservation of sage-grouse habitat.

Data collected over the long term provide the sturdiest foundation for basing management decisions. Utah has been conducting range trend studies in sagebrush and shrub-steppe habitats for over 20 years with Wildlife Restoration Act funds. These data provide critical information on how species and habitats have been affected and where to focus key rehabilitation efforts. The data also played an important role in determining appropriate objective numbers for mule deer herds and helped settle a conflict between elk and livestock use of habitat.

Using a variety of grants in the Federal Assistance toolbox, the Western States are working together and individually to conserve an invaluable part of the heritage of the American West. Preserving these landscapes will reduce the risk of listing species as endangered and will benefit the American people.

Pronghorn antelope. USFWS

State Wildlife Grant Program Funds Critical Waterbird Inventory for South Dakota

A major priority for State Wildlife Grants funding is to help prevent future endangered species listings. Collecting baseline information on the status of wildlife species is a critical step. The South Dakota Department of Game, Fish and Parks (SDGFP) has used State Wildlife Grant funds to contract with the Rocky Mountain Bird Observatory (RMBO) to conduct a Statewide inventory of 44 waterbird species and to develop a monitoring system that SDGFP can use in future years to track the status of these species. The vast majority of these species are not included on the State or Federal lists of threatened or endangered species. The SDGFP hopes this project will detect potential problems with any of these species before they become too serious.

The project has been contracted to RMBO because of their expertise in developing and implementing bird monitoring systems. Results of the work have relevance to entities responsible for water quality, fisheries, and streambank and aquatic habitat protection. Of coincidental interest is the status of the double-crested cormorant in South Dakota, a species that has been blamed for game fish declines in other parts of the upper Midwest.

The 2005 field season yielded the following highlights: A list of 560 known breeding sites was assembled from both historical information and field visits; 408 of the sites were visited in 2005. Sites with the highest number of breeding waterbird species or populations included Bitter Lake in Day County, Goose Lake in Codington County, LaCreek National Wildlife Refuge in Bennett County, and Sand Lake National Wildlife Refuge in Brown County.

Chad Tussing, South Dakota Game, Fish and Parks helps children attending the "Catch a Rainbow" program of aquatic education learn how to fish. Photo courtesy of South Dakota Game, Fish and Parks.

Catch a Rainbow

Catch a Rainbow is a fishing event designed for people with disabilities in residential facilities in Sioux Falls, South Dakota. The 2006 Catch a Rainbow was the 18th year of the event attracting about 600 people in 4 days.

Prior to the swimming pool's summer season, the local swimming pool is stocked with about 4,000 rainbow trout. The trout are supplied by a South Dakota Game, Fish & Parks (SDGFP) fish hatchery. Each angler can catch—and keep—up to 3 fish. The fish are then cleaned and iced for the anglers. Many of the participants have large fish feeds the same evening at their facilities. SDGFP staff, Outdoor Campus staff, and many volunteers clean fish, haul buckets, and assist the participants.

Aquatic education funds are used to purchase bait, purchase and maintain fishing equipment (which is also used for other programs), purchase t-shirts for volunteers, and provide staff hours at the event.

Members of the Minuteman Archery Club Range in Stoneville, South Dakota, prior to renovation of the building for hunter education classes and simulated hunting scenaros for students. Photo courtesy of South Dakota Game, Fish and Parks.

Cold War Relic Benefits Archers Through Hunter Education Program
The Minuteman Archery Club, located near Stoneville, South Dakota, has been working with the South Dakota Department of Game, Fish & Parks during the last 3 years to improve its archery range. This range is unique as it was formerly a Surplus Minuteman Missile Control Facility near the Village of Stoneville.

The Minuteman Archery Club has been renovating the facility to accommodate its use as an indoor archery. In 2004, the club repaired or renovated the largest facility, which will serve as the indoor archery range. In 2005, renovation continued with some sheetrocking and the purchase of bows, compressed carpet targets, and materials to construct a target stand and backstop with a lighted base. In 2006, the club is continuing renovations, building storage shelves, purchasing 3-D range targets, and maintaining the parking lot.

The archery range provides an opportunity for the residents of Stoneville and rural Meade County to learn and practice archery skills. This range also provides another recreational opportunity in a remote community.

*Upper Yellowstone River
Basin Cutthroat Research —
State Wildlife Grants*
The last remaining refugia for pure
Yellowstone cutthroat trout (YSC),
under Wyoming Game and Fish
Department jurisdiction, are in the
upper Yellowstone River basin. Due to
the remote location of the Yellowstone
River upstream of Yellowstone Lake, no
systematic inventory of cutthroat trout
has been conducted. Several new threats
jeopardizing the YSC in the Yellowstone
River basin include lake trout recently
introduced into Yellowstone Lake,
whirling disease found in some
Yellowstone Lake tributaries, and the
introduction of New Zealand Mud snails
in nearby drainages. All of these threats
have the potential to negatively impact
native cutthroat trout populations in the
upper Yellowstone River watershed. The
work completed under a State Wildlife
Grant was directed toward determination
of seasonal movement patterns and
macrohabitat use of YSC within the
drainage and a basin wide survey of the
Yellowstone River upstream from the
confluence of Thorofare Creek.

To find answers to the habits of the
YSC, 152 fish were implanted with radio
transmitters to track their movement by
aerial and ground monitoring methods. A
total of 605 individual YSC locations were
documented including capture locations,
aerial telemetry locations, and ground
telemetry locations. After 2 years of
study, the fish movement was determined
to be a highly mobile spawning population
with one resident population verified to
date. One of the interesting results of the
monitoring showed that the spawning
run appears to begin quite early in the
spring—possibly when ice cover is still on
Yellowstone Lake.

Habitat site utilization was recorded for
future ground truthing and measurement
of habitat characteristics. During three
sampling trips, physical characteristics
of numerous main stem and tributary
streams were classified using the
Wyoming Habitat Assessment Method
(WHAM) and stream habitat features

measured. Level-one WHAMs were
conducted on all 11 major tributaries
in the Yellowstone River drainage
upstream from the confluence with
Thorofare Creek. Habitat features
such as stream substrate type, riparian
condition, barriers to fish migration and
upland habitat condition were recorded.
In addition, site scale and watershed
scale habitat attributes were collected
to conduct YSC presence probability
modeling. Barriers to fish movement
were located and YSC distribution was
disseminated for future entry into the
YSC Risk Assessment database.

The sampling corroborated the telemetry
findings. Very few adult YSC remain in
the upper Yellowstone River tributaries
later than July. The lack of adult YSC
present suggests that YSC inhabiting
the upper Yellowstone River tributaries
are almost entirely adfluvial. Only three
resident populations were observed.
Juvenile YSC emerge from gravels from
late June through August. The juveniles
reside in the stream for up to 3 years
before immigrating to Yellowstone Lake.
Neither New Zealand mud snails nor
Whirling Disease were found in the
Yellowstone River tributaries above the
Thorofare River.

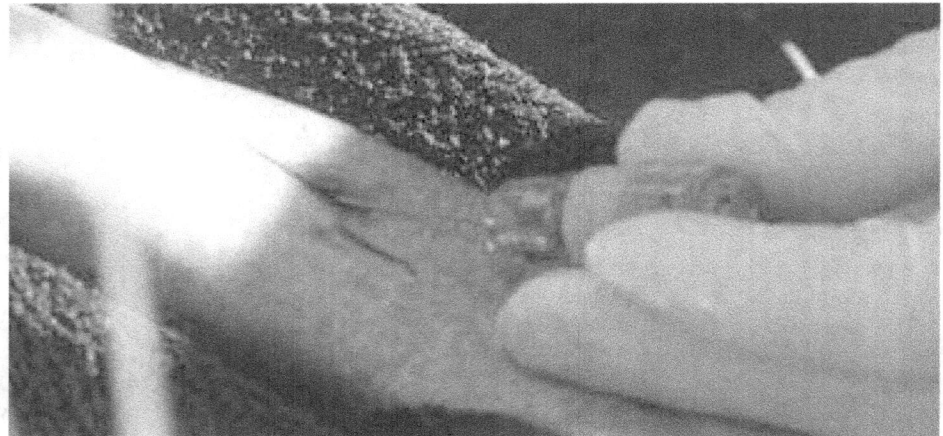

Yellowstone cutthroat trout being fitted with radio transmitter.

Locating Yellowstone cutthroat trout in the upper Yellowstone River basin.

Paddlefish and Others Benefit from Sport Fish Restoration Program
The Missouri River Ecology Project involves long-term monitoring and research of fish populations and their habitats in unchannelized and channelized reaches of the Missouri River bordering Nebraska. This project has resulted in a large, long-term data base that is used to develop management recommendations by the Nebraska Game and Parks Commission to fulfill its public trust responsibilities. This database has also been used to develop statistical models relating biotic responses to variables such as discharge, temperature, and turbidity from Ft. Randall Dam, South Dakota downstream to Rulo, Nebraska. Results suggest that more natural flow, temperature, and turbidity regimes would benefit native fish and invertebrate species in the Missouri River. These results will also be used in the adaptive management process adopted by the U.S. Army Corps of Engineers and the U.S. Fish and Wildlife Service for recovery of the Missouri River.

Paddlefish population data from this study has been incorporated into the Mississippi Interstate Cooperative Resource Association's multi-State, multi-jurisdictional paddlefish study completed in 2005. The study assessed the condition of paddlefish stocks in the lower Missouri River Basin. This project also provided the data necessary for the Nebraska Game and Parks Commission and the South Dakota Department of Game, Fish and Parks to jointly manage a sport harvest season for paddlefish in a reach of Missouri River below Gavins Point Dam. Results from this study were used to recommend a protective slot length limit and a harvest quota for sustainable management of this population.

Soon to be released are the results of a Missouri River public use assessment survey completed through a cooperative effort between the Missouri Department of Conservation and the Nebraska Game and Parks Commission. This public use survey was conducted on the Missouri River from Gavins Point Dam downstream 811 miles to the mouth of the Missouri at St. Louis, Missouri. This is the largest recreational user survey ever attempted in the Midwest. This study will not only provide information on the number of users and their activities, but will also measure the economic value that public users place on this resource using the Travel Cost and Contingent Value methodologies. This social-economic information is vital in any attempt to develop long-term management plans for the Missouri River.

Historically the Missouri River was one of the most dynamic large rivers in North America. This is one of many projects along the Missouri River corridor underway by the Nebraska Game and Parks Commission and various partners.

Paddlefish captured with seines, as part of a multi-state, multi-juridictional study of the lower Missouri River, Nebraska Game and Parks Commission.   Photo courtesy of Nebraska Game and Parks Commission.

Wildlife Restoration Section 10 Funds Assist in Improving Access to Shooting Sports in Nebraska

Developed in 2004, the Nebraska Shooting Range Grant Assistance Program has been instrumental in providing needed funds to Nebraska shooting ranges. The bulk of the shooting range support for Nebraska hunters comes from club-style ranges that rely on volunteer labor and donations to maintain viability. The addition of Hunter Education Section 10 funds has been instrumental in enhancing Statewide public access to safe and family friendly range facilities. The range facilities also provide hunter education students a place to practice and improve their shooting skills. Since the inception of the program 20 projects have been funded with $333,547 and include firearm and archery ranges. Funded activities include construction of trap and skeet houses, berms, outdoor lights, range sidewalks, overhead baffles, education classrooms, equipment storage, and archery ranges. Funding has also assisted in purchasing associated equipment and includes 3-D archery targets, bows, target arrows, and skeet throwers.

In the community of Doniphan, the range program assisted with the Nebraska State Trap Association to renovate 24 trap houses and trap throwers at the Doniphan Trap Range. The range is host to the State Trap Shooting Championship competition that included 1,700 student competitors in 2006. A new trap house with thrower was constructed in the town of Cody to allow students to practice their shotgun shooting skill. Over 30 percent of the high school and junior high students are involved in the Nebraska State Trap Association competitive trap program that takes place in Doniphan. New and renovated archery ranges were constructed at Ponca State Park, Lower Big Blue Natural Resource District, and the City of Lincoln. Other communities receiving funds for shooting range improvements include Kearney, Crawford, Mitchell, Omaha, Fremont, York, Grand Island, Fremont, Crete, Papillion, and Jefferson County. As a result of the program, citizens in Nebraska are finding more opportunities to participate in shooting sports activities.

Nebraska Landowner Incentive Program Tallgrass Prairie Restoration

The tallgrass prairie, a critically imperiled ecosystem, is home to the Federally threatened western prairie-fringed orchid and vulnerable species such as the Iowa skipper, Otto skipper, regal fritillary, and massasauga rattlesnake. Historically, habitat conversion to cropland has been the greatest threat to this ecosystem. However, degradation of remaining prairies due to inadequate management practices and invasive plants now takes precedence.

Nebraska is using the Landowner Incentive Program (LIP) to connect with private landowners in order to rejuvenate unbroken tallgrass prairies and guide ecologically and economically sustainable management. The promoted tools for tallgrass prairie management include intensive prescribed grazing, extensive periods of rest from grazing, and prescribed burning. Appropriate management is encouraged through landowner seminars, personal consultations, and cost-share projects that support a diversity of native plant and wildlife habitats.

Hunters of all ages can practice and improved their archery skills on ranges constructed in natural settings. Photo courtesy of Nebraska Game and Parks Commission.

Through LIP, positive collaborations have developed between project coordinators and landowners. Those efforts have resulted in on-the-ground rare species habitat projects and respectful dialogue concerning rare species conservation. LIP cost-share projects have directly impacted nearly 10,000 acres of Nebraska tallgrass prairie through prescribed burning, invasive tree removal, and improved grazing management. To date, 45 cost-share projects have been completed and 160 landowners have received personal consultations concerning rare species and sustainable tallgrass management on their properties.

Nebraska's State Wildlife Grant Program Efforts Receive National Award for Scientific Excellence
In the Spring of 2006, the Nebraska Natural Heritage Program, funded with State Wildlife Grant Program funds, received the National Award for Scientific Excellence for its role in developing the scientific methodology and data products used in the Nebraska Natural Legacy Project. The program was selected for special recognition by NatureServe, the nonprofit conservation group that coordinated an international network of 80 similar natural heritage programs across the United States, Canada, and Latin America.

The Nebraska Natural Legacy Project is the first comprehensive plan ever developed for wildlife and plants in Nebraska. This planning effort was guided by a 20-member partnership team that included leaders from the conservation and agricultural community, nongovernmental organizations, and the Ponca Tribe of Nebraska. The partnership team represented many of the entities and individuals that likely would be involved with implementing the blueprint developed. Four informational meetings were held in each of 4 ecoregions across the State: Tallgrass Prairie, Mixed grass prairie, Shortgrass Prairie, and Sandhills. Information gathered at 16 public meetings was incorporated into the Legacy Plan.

The removal of non-native cedar trees and other woody vegetation from native grasslands in Nebraska, is allowing these grasslands to be restored and provide significant habitat for wildlife. Photo courtesy of Nebraska Game and Parks Commission.

Within the four ecoregions, biologically unique landscapes (BUL) were identified that offer some of the best opportunities for conserving the full array of biological diversity in Nebraska. After approval of the conservation strategy, the Nebraska Game and Parks Commission moved forward with additional public meetings within BULs where infrastructure is in place to begin cooperative projects. Projects within the tallgrass prairie include the Sandstone Prairies BUL, Verdigre-Bazille Watershed BUL, Loess Canyons BUL, and Central Loess Hills BUL which are in various stages of planning, development, and implementation. Within the Sandstone Prairies BUL and Verdigre-Bazille Watershed BUL, cooperative projects are underway in cooperation with Natural Resources Conservation Service, University of Nebraska at Lincoln extension offices, Farm Service Agency, Nature Conservancy, Natural Resource Districts, and various other partners.

The initial 20-member partnership team has determined the group will remain intact and continue to promote integration of the Legacy Plan in activities across the State. Current projects undertaken by the Nebraska Game and Parks, focused by the Legacy Plan, include Salt Creek Tiger Beetle research and saline wetland restoration; American Burying Beetle research and land acquisition; Massasauga research; and Landowner Incentive Program private land restoration projects in the Tallgrass, Shortgrass, and Mixed Grass areas.

Salt Creek Tiger Beetle. USFWS

A service botanist looks after an endangered Western Prairie Fringed Orchid in Nebraska. Fringed orchids are found in tallgrass prairies, most often in moist habitats or sedge meadows, and require direct sunlight for growth. They persist in areas disturbed by light grazing, burning, or mowing. Western Prairie Fringed Orchids are known from northeastern Oklahoma, as well as locations in Kansas, Missouri, Nebraska, Iowa, Minnesota, and South Dakota. The greatest threat to the species is conversion of tallgrass prairie to other land uses. Hollingsworth/USFWS

In 2002, Montana began receiving funding from the USFWS to address species with unmet conservation needs through State Wildlife Grants (SWG). These funds support conservation projects for species of greatest conservation need, meaning those for which biological information is lacking, whose populations are in decline, or that are at risk for decline. Through this program, Montana has been able to begin to address a number of fisheries and wildlife conservation needs that otherwise would have gone unmet. The "Native Prairie Fish Survey and Inventory" and the "Statewide Small Mammal Survey and Inventory" constitute 2 important projects undertaken by Montana Fish, Wildlife and Parks (MFWP) with State Wildlife Grants funds. These projects are consistent with Montana's recently approved Comprehensive Wildlife Conservation Strategy.

State Wildlife Grant Program Assist Essential Native Fish Survey and Inventory
An analysis of Montana Fish, Wildlife and Park's (MFWP) Montana River Information System (MRIS) database in 2002 revealed that more than 4,200 streams comprising more than 18,000 stream miles (18 percent of the mapped stream miles in Montana) had never been surveyed. The overwhelming majority of these waters are small warm-water prairie streams located in the eastern half of the State. Although these streams offer little or no potential as a sport fishery, there is a strong likelihood that many of them contain intact, diverse assemblages of native fish, reptiles and amphibian species, at least during parts of the year. A need existed to survey these prairie streams to gain a greater understanding of the fisheries and fauna that occur there. This baseline data would be critical in enabling resource managers to better understand and manage prairie species and their habitats.

Since then, SWG funding has been used to survey hundreds of never-before-surveyed prairie streams and riparian

habitat in Montana's prairie region. The third year of surveys was completed in 2005 when 515 sites were visited. Forty-three percent of the sites sampled were on private property. The remaining sites were located on State of Montana, Bureau of Land Management (BLM), United States Fish and Wildlife Service, or National Forest Service lands. Of the 515 sites, 285 were dry and 230 had water. Fish were sampled at 170 of the wet sites and no fish were found at the remaining 60 streams.

During 2005 surveys, 62,148 individual fish representing 41 different species were documented. Twenty-five of the species are native to Montana and the remaining 16 are introduced. The common carp was the most commonly encountered introduced fish (35 sites) followed by the black bullhead (23 sites) and green sunfish (21) sites. The fathead minnow was the most highly distributed fish, being sampled in 129 sites or 76 percent of the locations. The mean number of fish species per site was 4.8 with the range numbering between 1 and 17 species per site. The most abundant species sampled was the fathead minnow, accounting for 36.3 percent of all fish sampled. The brook stickleback and plains minnow were the next most abundant species, making up 7.26 percent and 7.13 percent of the individuals sampled, respectively.

A black bullhead captured during seining of prairie streams in Montana. Photo courtesy of Montana Fish, Wildlife and Parks.

Stream teams seining a prairie stream in eastern Montana. Photo courtesy of Montana Fish, Wildlife and Parks.

Montana Region 4's Teton River had 17 fish species documented which was the largest number of fish species found at a single site. The greatest number of individual fish recorded at a single site was 5,722 at Region 4's Horse Thief Coulee. Arrow Creek followed with 3,840 individual fish, consisting of 14 species. Thirty-five of the streams contained 500 or more fish. Forty-seven percent of the sites had 5 or more species of fish, while the remaining 53 percent contained 4 or fewer species. Thirty-three sites contained only one species of fish including the fathead minnow at 42 percent of the sites and the brook stickleback at 12 percent of the sites.

State Wildlife Grant Funds Benefiting Shrews, Voles and Jumping Mouse
Small mammals, including shrew, voles, and mice, are some of the least understood species groups in Montana. While Montana Fish Wildlife and Parks (MFWP) and other agencies conducted prior surveys, a thorough and concerted effort was needed to survey these species across Montana's broad spectrum of habitats. In 2004, MFWP initiated a 3-year inventory project to provide a current assessment of the occurrence, status, and distribution of small mammals across the State.

Focusing on areas that had received little historic sampling effort, three survey crews targeted MFWP lands while conducting stratified random sampling of habitats on surrounding lands. Sampling priority was given to those areas and habitats with little to no historical information on the small mammal community. Trapping lines were the primary survey technique with additional supplemental observations and surveys providing data on other species groups including bats, amphibians, reptiles, and birds.

Crews started in eastern Montana and will finish surveying the western portion of the State this summer. With half of the 2006 season completed, crews have documented 27 of the 32 small mammal species known to occur in Montana and

Northern Short-tailed shrew. Photo courtesy of Phil Myers, University of Michigan

expect more to be added before the season concludes. Highlights include a new species, the first documented occurrence of the Northern Short-tailed shrew in northeastern Montana; data from 20 Arctic Shrews across 3 locations, a species previously only recorded at one location; significant records for the following Montana Species of Concern — Sagebrush vole, Merriam's shrew, Pygmy shrew, Hayden's shrew, and Meadow jumping mouse. The project has generated data on 5,010 individual captures and 2,100 miscellaneous observations of 240 species. These data are a great resource for future species distribution updates, baseline habitat associations, Species of Concern status reviews, and habitat conservation efforts.

Bull River/Lake Creek Habitat Conservation Plan Acquisition
In 1996, Plum Creek Timber Company (PCTC) began evaluating its land holdings along rivers, wetlands and streams in northwestern Montana and has since classified some of these holdings as "Higher and Better Use" lands—or lands that have higher real estate value than they do for timber production. Montana Fish, Wildlife & Parks (MFWP), along with other agencies and organizations, have since worked cooperatively with PCTC to conserve the most critical of these lands and to keep these valuable resources in public ownership. One such parcel, known as the Bull River/Lake Creek complex, was identified by MFWP as its highest priority for 2004 Habitat Conservation Plan Land Acquisition (HCPLA) Grant funding.

Prior to this, the State of Montana had identified the Bull River as core bull trout habitat and a priority watershed for protection and restoration of west-slope cutthroat trout, a "species of special concern." The State also established a long-term goal to protect and restore existing bull trout and west-slope cutthroat trout populations and associated habitats in the Bull River and Lake Creek watersheds.

A view of the Bull River & Lake Creek Habitat Conservation Acquisition from the Plum Creek Timber Company by Montana Fish, Wildlife and Parks, using U.S. Fish and Wildlife Service, Endangered Species grant funds. The Division of Federal Assistance administers and manages these grant awards in coordination with the Division of Ecological Services. Photo courtesy of Montana Fish, Wildlife and Parks.

In February of 2005, through a combined effort involving MFWP, USFWS, PCTC, the Avista Corporation and The Conservation Fund, over 1,800 acres of critical habitat within the Bull River/ Lake Creek Complex were transferred to MFWP creating what is now the Bull River Wildlife Management Area. The site includes 1,285 acres that were acquired with proceeds from a Habitat Conservation Plan Land Acquisition awarded to MFWP, along with a 40-acre fee-title and 561-acre conservation easement donation by the Avista Corporation.

Tim Bodurtha, Supervisor in the USFWS office in Kalispell, Montana, captured the significance of the accomplishment: *"The creation of the Bull River Wildlife Management Area is a great example of how the HCP Land Acquisition Grant Program has worked in Montana. Through the efforts of a dedicated and diverse group of partners, we have conserved one of the most wildlife-rich areas in the Bull River Valley for future generations."*

Landowner Incentive Program and State Wildlife Grant Program benefits Tribal Conservation Efforts
The U.S. Fish and Wildlife Service has awarded competitive grants to 19 Tribes in Region 6 totaling $7,741,319, since 2003. There have been 24 Tribal Wildlife Grants (TWG – $4.9 million in Federal funds and $1.4 million in matching tribal funds) and 20 Tribal Landowner Incentive Program (TLIP – $2.8 million in Federal funds and $1.2 million in matching tribal funds) awarded.

These competitive grants are used for a variety of projects including: wildlife surveys, inventories and associated projects for mammals and furbearers, black-footed ferrets, swift fox, grizzly bears, wolves, and sage-grouse; landowner stream restoration projects for riparian and wetland creation and restoration, noxious weed control and prairie vegetation restoration; development of comprehensive fish and wildlife management plans, including land use plans for native and endangered species; acquisition of lands for wetland and riparian restoration to benefit native fish and grizzly bear habitat; and various riverine endangered species habitat developments and implementation of management plans for fish and wildlife.

Two examples of completed grant proposals:

The Lower Brule Sioux Tribe in South Dakota was awarded a grant to restore 10 wetlands totaling 40 acres and to create 10 wetlands totaling 60 acres on the Lower Brule Reservation in South Dakota. Creation and restoration of wetland habitat will benefit high priority species identified in the North American Wetlands Conservation Act (NAWCA).

The Confederated Salish and Kootenai Tribes of the Flathead Nation in Montana were awarded a grant to study habitat suitability for the possible reintroduction of the Columbia sharp-tailed grouse, an animal of high cultural significance to the tribes. A strong native grassland component still exists even though much of the study area is impacted by cheatgrass, spotted knapweed and grazing. Overall, exotic species were present at low percentages. The study found that winter and nesting habitat are spatially segregated and that only 5 percent of the study area contains winter habitat. Overall, the study showed a very limited amount of area currently suitable for the grouse. The study identified changes in current management practices, such as fencing of riparian zones from cattle use. The results of the study will be used to increase the probability of successful reintroduction of the Columbia sharp-tailed grouse.

Sharp-tailed grouse. Bob Hines/USFWS

*Sport Fish Restoration Program
Improves Fishing Access*

The Colorado Division of Wildlife established the "Fishing Is Fun" program almost 20 years ago to create local partnerships for the improvement of angling throughout Colorado. Since then, the Fishing Is Fun (FIF) program has funded more than 200 angling improvement projects at rivers, streams, ponds and lakes utilizing Sport Fish Restoration Program funds and local matching dollars. Local match has averaged about 45 percent of total project costs over the years, nearly doubling the impact of Sport Fish Restoration Program funds.

An example of FIF's success lies in the Town of the Silverthorne which is located about 60 miles west of Denver and is a gateway to many diverse mountain recreation opportunities. The Blue River, a "Colorado Gold Medal Fishery," flows through Silverthorne. It is noted for its year-round fishing opportunities and scenic beauty. As a result, it receives heavy fishing pressure and other impacts associated with human use. To address this, the town applied to the Fishing Is Fun program in 2004 for $120,000 to improve fish habitat and angling access along a three-quarter-mile stretch of the river.

The town completed the project in September 2005. Habitat improvements included the installation of boulder habitat clusters, shrub pockets, and instream riffle/pool/glide sequences. Angler access points were installed along 3,000 feet of the access trail. These improvements now allow anglers to move beyond the upper section of the Blue River in Silverthorne, reducing crowding and dispersing angling pressure on the river. It also provides anglers and others with access to a scenic stretch of river in an urban setting. As a local outdoor writer described it, the project gave "one of the most gorgeous rivers in all of Colorado... a fishing-friendly face-lift" for the benefit of all.

*Riverine restoration on the Blue River in Silverthorne, Colorado.
Photo courtesy of Colorado Division of Wildlife.*

The Colorado Aquatic Animal Health Program - Federal Aid Sport Fish Restoration

The Colorado Division of Wildlife (CDOW) Aquatic Animal Health Program assists in the protection, conservation, and management of Colorado's aquatic animal resources through the monitoring, investigation, and management of aquatic animal health in State fish hatcheries, research facilities, free-ranging public fisheries and free-ranging aquatic animal populations. CDOW also provides diagnostics, research, regulated pathogen inspections, and laboratory analysis for aquatic animal resources in the private sector. Aquatic animal health services and management are an essential and integral part of agency efforts to protect, enhance, and restore Colorado's aquatic resources. Maintaining or improving aquatic animal health helps insure the stability of many populations, enable the recovery of others, and improve the quality of Colorado's wildlife resources.

Using Federal Aid in Sport Fish Restoration Act funds, the CDOW Aquatic Animal Health Program conducts the following aquatic resource health activities:

■ All agency fish health services including diagnostics, regulated pathogen inspections, and extension services to CDOW's 23 fish culture facilities and 17 subunits, the State's wild fisheries, and more than 35 licensed commercial aquaculture facilities (licensed under the Department of Agriculture) across the State of Colorado.

■ All fish pathogen analyses, molecular probes, and expertise for CDOW fishery researchers, as well as, independent fish health investigation and research.

■ Support and leadership in the formulation of fish disease management plans, policies, and regulations to effectively protect Colorado's wildlife resources.

■ Monitor and ensure regulatory compliance with fish health regulations.

Colorado Combines LIP and SWG Funds to Benefit Plovers, Owls, Eagles and Frogs

The CDOW Aquatic Animal Health Program consists of seven permanent employees operating from laboratories and headquarters in Brush, Colorado. The unit serves Colorado's free-ranging fishery resources, as well as public and private fish culture. Our staff works on some 300 fish health cases a year, including regulated salmonid disease inspections, diagnostics, fish health surveys, research analysis, and forensics. In addition, biologists from the unit provide guidance in setting fish health regulations and policies and provide input on the issuance and enforcement of Aquatic Species Importation Licenses, Aquaculture Permits, and related permits. Special projects include a Statewide survey of Aquatic Nuisance Species and regular monitoring of hatchery fish quality.

Wineinger-Davis Ranch, Lincoln County, Colorado – LIP and SWG in Colorado

The Colorado Division of Wildlife (CDOW) acquired a conservation easement of over 11,240 acres of native shortgrass prairie and riparian habitat in Southeastern Colorado. These habitats and associated wildlife have declined due to impacts from conversion of prairie to agricultural, commercial, and residential housing development. The easement will provide permanent protection of shortgrass prairie habitat and associated Colorado wildlife species of concern, while agricultural operations continue on the Wineinger-Davis Ranch. Species which will benefit include mountain plovers, Plains leopard frogs, burrowing owls, swift fox, Massasauga snakes, ferruginous hawks, and bald eagles.

The Wineinger-Davis family applied for the conservation easement through the Colorado Species Conservation Partnership Program (CSCP) established by the CDOW. CSCP funding is derived through Great Outdoors Colorado lottery proceeds, Landowner Incentive Program funding, State Wildlife Grant funding, and landowner match. The CSCP engages in cooperative efforts to prevent the further decline of Colorado's wildlife species of concern, meet species conservation goals of declining species in the State, reduce the necessity of listing of species under the Endangered Species Act, and to down-list or delist threatened and endangered species.

A view of the Wineinger-Davis Ranch Conservation Easement in southeastern Colorado. Photo courtesy of Colorado Division of Wildlife.

Sport Fish Restoration Funds Improve Local Access Sites and Fisheries

Community Fisheries Assistance Program (CFAP)

Prior to 2005, the Kansas Department of Wildlife and Parks (KDWP) conducted surveys that indicated more than 25 percent of the State's anglers preferred to fish in small impoundments. The survey also showed that approximately 120 communities in the State operated about 220 bodies of water for public fishing access. Nearly half of these waters, however, required a local fee for fishing in addition to the purchase of a Kansas State Fishing License. Many locations also required a fee for boating, general access, or both. To remedy this, the KDWP introduced the Community Fisheries Assistance Program (CFAP) in 2005 to increase access to quality fishing opportunities across Kansas.

CFAP is an ongoing program which partners with cities, counties, and public entities to enhance recreational fishing opportunities and aquatic resources by leasing the angling rights. The program targets community lakes because of their popularity with anglers and the convenience of fishing close to home. Many community lakes provide fishing opportunities to urban residents and rural anglers, while serving all socioeconomic groups.

As smaller impoundments were generally constructed for purposes other than fishing, local participation also includes KDWP assistance with fisheries management, supplemental stockings, and angling facilities to further enhance fishing access and success. CFAP participants receive an annual lease payment; 75 percent of which must be spent to operate and maintain the fishery for anglers. This helped to eliminate local permit fees on approximately 90 percent of the waters targeted by CFAP in 2005.

To date, 115 communities have enrolled 203 lakes in the program totaling over 12,000 acres of water. Participating communities were contacted at the end of

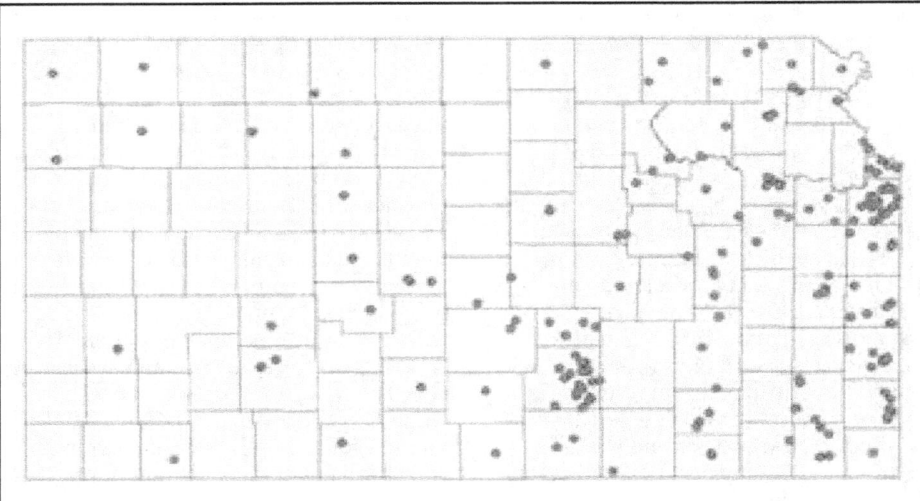

Community Fisheries Assistance locations in Kansas.

2005 for their evaluation of the program. Nearly half of the program participants reported increased number of anglers. Overall satisfaction with the program was rated as good to excellent, as was the effectiveness of the program in increasing opportunities for anglers.

Program costs totaled approximately $1 million for 2005 with local contributions totaling $267,556 and Federal Aid in Sport Fish Restoration funds amounting to $802,669 making this program 100 percent reimbursable with no out-of-pocket expense to the State. Communities involved with CFAP have shown a true financial dedication to fisheries management and have helped create successful partnerships between Federal, State, and local governments while increasing fishing access and opportunity in Kansas.

Studying Distribution and Status of Amphibians, Reptiles, and Turtles in Kansas

For a number of years, biologists at the Kansas Department of Wildlife and Parks (KDWP) recognized a need for a study of the State's herpetofauna. Herps are poorly understood compared with other vertebrate groups in the State. Relatively few studies have been conducted on the status of amphibians,

reptiles, and turtles in Kansas and the protection of prairie herpetofauna has not received much attention. Fortunately, Congress authorized the State Wildlife Grants (SWG) program in 2001 and appropriated money for State fish and game agencies to focus on "species of greatest conservation need." Given this opportunity, the KDWP began a project in 2003 to study the distribution and status of herpetofauna in Kansas.

Using SWG funds, the KDWP contracted with a State university to survey these important species for future research and conservation efforts. The study extended Statewide and focused on 5 objectives: 1) the identification of new localities for imperiled species; 2) the determination of population status estimates for imperiled species; 3) the characterization of habitat preferences for imperiled species; 4) the collection and curation of tissues of Kansas' amphibians, reptiles, and turtles; and 5) the construction of an online database system to serve both management and education users.

The project was completed in 2005. Among the results, the survey recorded 14,831 new occurrences of amphibians, reptiles, and turtles in Kansas collected from 4,046 unique sites. Site, latitude, longitude, date, and time of collection were recorded for each occurrence. Approximately 23 percent of the specimens have been preserved as museum vouchers and the remainders are in the form of the recorded observation described above. The project data was combined with previously collected data in a Geographic Information System to characterize each species' general habitat. An on-line accessible database (the Kansas Herp Atlas; available at http://webcat.fhsu. edu/ksfauna/herps) was created to store all project data. The website is useful for both general education and wildlife management.

The survey information has given KDWP biologists a greater understanding of the distribution and natural history of Kansas herpetofauna, contributing to a long-term goal of identifying species in "greatest need of information." Findings will also provide additional support for policy directives, regulatory decisions, and species management. The internet-based database system will provide instantaneous access of data by wildlife officials, managers, and researchers.

Seining for amphibians, reptiles and turtles in an intermittent flow stream in Kansas. Photo courtesy of Kansas Department of Wildlife and Parks.

Community Fisheries Assistance completed project with a floating fishing pier in Kansas. Photo courtesy of Kansas Department of Wildlife and Parks.

Looking for signs of reproduction, including eggs and juveniles of amphibians, reptiles and turtles in a sample of pooled stream water in Kansas. Photo courtesy of Kansas Department of Wildlife and Parks.

A group of snakes found in one location of the amphibian, reptile and turtle survey in Kansas. Photo courtesy of Kansas Department of Wildlife and Parks.

Wildlife Restoration Program Opens 125,000 Acres of Private Land to Hunters
As the population continues to become more urban, fewer Kansas residents have easy access to land for hunting. In addition, there's very little public land in Kansas. Only 340,000 acres (or 0.6 percent) of Kansas land and water are owned or managed by the Kansas Department of Wildlife and Parks (KDWP). Of these 340,000 acres, only 277,000 are open to public hunting. Of additional concern, there is a growing trend for landowners to lease their properties for private hunting, which further reduces available public access for urban residents. This shortage of hunting access has been identified as the major factor in the decline in hunting, and consequently, hunting license sales.

The KDWP established the Walk-In-Hunting Access Program (WIHA) to address public hunting access. Since its inception in 1994, WIHA has proven to be very successful. Annually, over 2,000 landowners have enrolled more than 1 million acres in 101 of the State's 105 counties for the fall WIHA season; during the spring turkey portion of the program, more than 125,000 acres in 60 counties have been leased. Landowner response continues to exceed expectations for both fall WIHA and spring turkey hunting access properties. As response has increased, the type of habitat cover enrolled continues to diversify. Waterfowl feeding areas, rangeland, and riparian areas are becoming available and readily utilized by constituents.

As part of the program, approximately 130,000 atlases are produced annually for the fall season and an additional 35,000 copies are printed for the spring turkey season. The atlases show the location of the tracts and the regulations that apply to each area. An atlas index lists the major game species likely to be encountered on each tract which enables hunters to select the areas according to their hunting preferences. Atlases are also available to constituents over the KDWP Web site in downloadable and printable formats.

A young hunter in the walk-in hunting area brings home a turkey. Photo courtesy of Kansas Department of Wildlife and Parks.

Juveniles hunting pheasant with their dog, display the results of their hunting success on private land. Their hunting experience was made possible through the Kansas Hunting Access to Private Land, through the use of Wildlife Restoration Act funds. Photo courtesy of Kansas Department of Wildlife and Parks.

Hunter Education Funds Warm Up North Dakota Winters

When the Minot Rifle and Pistol Club purchased a 120-acre parcel of land for an outdoor shooting range, they dreamed of one day building an indoor state-of-the-art 25-meter gun range. The winter climate on the plains of North Dakota allows use of the outdoor range for only a few months of the year, while the addition of an indoor range would provide year-round enjoyment.

With the help of a grant from the North Dakota Game and Fish Department under the Wildlife Restoration Act, this group of 500 shooting enthusiasts rallied their forces and built their dream. The indoor shooting range facility has a classroom, an Action Target backstop that will handle most calibers, and is set up to facilitate use by folks with disabilities. This collaboration has provided a safe, functional, and suitable structure to shoot firearms for many generations to come.

State Wildlife Grant Program Helps with Pelican Mystery

The white pelicans of Chase Lake are disappearing by the thousands and no one knows why. Over 4 days in May of 2004, the number of white pelicans at the lake dropped from 27,000 to 80, and thousands of eggs and chicks were left unattended and dying. In 2005, 18,000 adult pelicans returned to Chase Lake for nesting. Everything seemed to have returned to normal until July, when dead white pelican chicks were discovered — 8,000 at last count — and the adults again abandoned the area. State Wildlife Grants are being used to help unravel this mystery, as well as to gather basic data on white pelican behavior. Understanding why these birds are disappearing is important to us all, because the health of wildlife can be an early indicator of disease and pollution that affect us all.

Dakota Waters Boating Access in North Dakota. Photo courtesy of North Dakota Game and Fish Department.

Boating Access— Come Drought or High Water

Tourism and recreation is North Dakota's second largest industry. Fishing and boating are an integral and important part of everyday life. Although North Dakota's population has remained relatively stable, fishing license sales and boat registration numbers are up significantly. As a result, excitement and participation in fishing and boating have surged and the sporting public is demanding the development of additional facilities to help meet those needs.

The North Dakota Game and Fish Department continues to coordinate and work with local interests in developing and upgrading a wide variety of boating and fishing related facilities at more than 250 recreation lakes throughout the State. The Department's "Fisheries Development Out-Grant Program" has proven to be an effective system in administering Federal Aid from the Sport Fish Restoration Program to local communities. Through cooperative

efforts with local partners, the department provides more than a million dollars annually to construct, upgrade and maintain facilities.

The success of this cost-share program is due largely to the involvement and cooperation of the local communities who volunteer thousands of hours and work diligently to raise matching funds to construct and maintain these facilities. Many of the fishing waters are surrounded by private lands, and landowners almost always donate the land necessary for development of the boating access and recreation site. In recent years, the department has faced the challenge of providing access to drought-stricken waters in one part of the State while, at the same time, combating record high water levels in other parts.

Golden Eagles Benefit from State Wildlife Grant Program

The status of golden eagles in North Dakota is unclear, but many eagle nests in the State do not have eagles living in them. A U.S. Forest Service study of factors that might negatively affect nesting golden eagles on the grasslands was expanded with State Wildlife Grant money to include surrounding lands, making this the first comprehensive study on the subject. Information from this research project will allow biologists to determine the status of golden eagles and make informed wildlife management decisions, allowing the most cost-effective path to golden eagle conservation.

Golden eagle. USFWS

Section 6 Funds Preserve a Unique Corner of the World in Utah

In the southwestern corner of Utah, three unique ecoystems, the Mojave Desert, the Great Basin, and the Colorado Plateau, merge to provide a biologically rich and unique mixture of wildlife and vegetation in a setting of spectacular red desert and rock formations. Combine that with year-round sunshine and outstanding recreational opportunities and you get the second fastest growing city in the country—St. George. In 1996, Washington County and local communities recognized the need to preserve the natural resources that attract so many people to the area while allowing planned development. Working with the U.S. Fish and Wildlife Service, the communities produced the Washington County Habitat Conservation Plan and created the Red Cliffs Desert Reserve, a 62,000-acre

scenic wildlife reserve set aside to protect the Federally threatened desert tortoise and other rare and sensitive plants and animals. Just a tiny representation of the diversity of the animals found in this Reserve includes the kit fox, mule deer, gila monster, chuckwalla, bald eagle, and Virgin River chub. The Reserve also supports habitat for the Federally listed southwestern willow flycatcher and Mexican spotted owl.

Utah, working in collaboration with the States of Nevada, Arizona, and California, identified other key habitats outside the Reserve that need protection. The unprecedented growth in the area has caused land prices to skyrocket, so Utah tapped into a grant program under the Endangered Species Act to help supplement the Reserve with fee title acquisitions and conservation easements protecting another 1,350 acres of habitat.

Desert tortoise on the Red Desert Reserve in Utah. USFWS

Desert tortoise habitat at the Red Desert Reserve, Utah. USFWS

Landowner Incentive Program Funds Assist with Conserving Ranching and Sagebrush Habitat

The Selman Ranch property, located in the foothills of Utah's Wasatch Mountains, consists of 6,722 acres of sagebrush grasslands and old growth Douglas-fir forest. It provides important habitat for Columbian sharp-tailed grouse, Bonneville cutthroat trout, northern goshawks, at least 5 species of bats, and several migratory bird species. The property also provides 4,300 acres of crucial winter habitat for mule deer and elk. A conservation easement has been established with the landowner to protect in perpetuity the significant agricultural, natural, and open space values of this property.

In an unusual twist, the Utah Department of Agriculture, rather than the State wildlife agency, is holding the conservation easement. Grazing and pasturing of livestock will continue on the ranch, using best management practices to maintain or improve habitat conditions. Pesticides will be allowed to control noxious weeds that compete against both agricultural crops and native vegetation. This innovative approach marks the beginning of integrated ranch land protection and conservation in this part of Utah for the benefit of a variety of wildlife resources.

Pinyon-juniper control in Utah's Basin Range. Photo courtesy of UDWR.

Aerial seeding in Utah's Basin Range. Photo courtesy of UDWR.

Sensitive Species Program Implemented with State Wildlife Grant Program Funds

State Wildlife Grants in Utah are being used to conserve wildlife and vital natural areas by restoring habitat, monitoring and managing wildlife, and improving stewardship on both public and private lands. Five biologists, hired with State Wildlife Grant funds, participate in wildlife rehabilitation programs and research projects that will assist in providing cost-effective solutions to management questions. The biologists are also testing for West Nile Virus and other diseases. This project is allowing us to identify and prevent problems before they threaten wildlife, and because wildlife health can be an early indicator of disease and pollution that can affect humans as well.

Managing Dixie harrow habitat. DWR

Pygmy rabbit.